Guernsey and the

Guernsey, as a loyal part of the British Empire, supported Britain during the 1914-1918 war. This war became known as the 'Great War', the 'War to end all Wars', but it was just the first of two world wars fought during the 20th century.

Before 1914

In 1914 the British Empire stretched all around the world and included countries which we know today as New Zealand, Australia, India, Pakistan, much of South and East Africa, Canada and many far flung islands and territories. This Empire made Britain the most important country in the world at the start of the Twentieth century.

Other European countries, like France and Germany, had smaller empires.

The colonies and territories which made up an empire brought wealth and prestige, providing cheap raw materials for the 'mother country' and a ready market for finished goods. The colonies themselves were introduced to such 'civilised' things as European-style government and laws, railways, postal services and taxation.

Britain's Empire and trade were protected by the Royal Navy. In the early part of the 20th century a newly unified Germany posed a threat to Britain when it began to build a sea-going fleet. The French feared the Germans, who had taken Alsace and Lorraine from France in 1871, and Russia was concerned that Germany wanted to take over some of its lands for the growing German population.

The 'Tri

Britain ... informal alliance - the 'Entente Cordiale' and asked Russia to join them. Russia's territories stretched from Europe to the Pacific and she had an army of millions of men. The 'Triple Entente', as they now became, had their potential enemy, Germany, surrounded.

The 'Central Powers'

Germany's main ally was Austria-Hungary (today's Austria, Hungary, Bosnia, Croatia and Slovakia) and initially, Italy. In the Middle East, they were also supported by countries known today as Turkey, Syria, Lebanon, Iraq and Jordan which formed the Ottoman (Turkish) Empire.

Countries like Greece, Albania, Serbia, Romania and Bulgaria were the Balkan States. They distrusted each other and resented Austria-Hungary, the Russians and the Turks.

The great German statesman, Bismarck, said

> **'If there is ever another war in Europe, it will come from some damned silly thing in the Balkans'.**

He was right...

Countdown to the Great War

Sunday 8th June, 1914

Archduke Franz Ferdinand, heir to the Austria-Hungary throne visited Sarajevo, the capital of Bosnia. Gavrilo Princip, a student from Serbia, shot and killed the Archduke and his wife. These shots effectively triggered the War.

July, 1914

Austria-Hungary accused Serbia of supporting Princip and sent a list of impossible demands. These would have meant the end of Serbia as a country so Serbia refused to accept them.

28th July, 1914

Austria-Hungary invaded Serbia. Russia supported 'little' Serbia.

1st August, 1914

Germany, in support of its ally, Austria-Hungary, declared war on Russia. France 'mobilised' (prepared her forces for war), in support of her ally Russia.

3rd August, 1914

Germany declared war on France and attacked through Belgium which was a 'neutral' country.

4th August, 1914

Britain declared war on Germany to support Belgium (as part of a treaty agreed in 1839) and to stop the Germans gaining control of the English Channel ports.

Who sided with whom?

The Triple Entente
(later The Allies)

Britain and her Empire including Australia, New Zealand, India, South Africa and Canada.

France and her Empire

Belgium

Japan

Portugal

The Russian Empire (until 1917)

The United States of America (from 1917)

Italy (after 1915)

Romania (after 1916)

Serbia

Montenegro

Greece (after 1917)

Brazil (after 1917)

Armenia (in 1918)

Other countries such as Andorra, Bolivia, Cuba, Ecuador, Haiti, Peru, San Marino and Uruguay were sympathetic to the Allied cause.

The Central Powers
(earlier The Triple Alliance)

Germany and her Empire

Austria-Hungary and her Empire

The Ottoman Empire (Turkey)

Italy (until 1915)

Bulgaria (from 1915)

Propaganda posters were used by all sides.

What they said: 1914

As Europe rumbled towards war Sir Edward Grey, the British foreign minister, looked out of his office window in London and seeing the lamplighter turning out the gas lights as dawn broke, said, **'The lights are going out all over Europe; we shall not see them lit again in our lifetime'**

'Just a scrap of paper' – the Kaiser and his generals did not think Britain would honour the agreement with Belgium. They were wrong.

'all be over by Christmas'

The French and German armies had a core of full-time professionals but most of the soldiers were conscripts. Conscripts had to do a period of army service by law in peacetime, then spend time in the 'reserves' and could be expected to be 'called up' in times of war. For France and Germany this could add up to 3.5 million men each.

Britain had never maintained a very big army, as her main fighting force was the Royal Navy. In 1914 the whole British Army had about 250,000 men. The British Expeditionary Force (BEF) of 100,000 men which went over to France in 1914 was a volunteer force, made up of soldiers who were spending at least 12 years in the Army. It was said to be the best army Britain has ever produced.

'The Old Contemptibles'

The Kaiser called the BEF 'a contemptible little army' so the BEF used the Kaiser's 'put-down' as a proud nickname! The original BEF are always referred to as 'The Old Contemptibles' – they even had a railway engine named after them!

There is a window in Guernsey's Town Church commemorating 'the Old Contemptibles'.

However, more men were needed and Lord Kitchener, the Secretary of State for War, thundered, 'Your Country needs You!'

All over Britain men rushed to volunteer and soon over one million were in training. The War was seen to be a great adventure and young men did not want to miss out on the fun; after all people were convinced that it would be **'all be over by Christmas'**.

BRITONS "WANTS" YOU JOIN YOUR COUNTRY'S ARMY! GOD SAVE THE KING

Reproduced by permission of LONDON OPINION

What they said: 1914

Sir Douglas Haig wrote in his diary of 4 August 1914 that
" **...Great Britain and Germany would be fighting for their existence. Therefore the war was bound to be a long war, and neither would admit defeat after a short struggle.**"

Germany's Problem

Germany was surrounded by France to the west and Russia to the east.

The German generals had foreseen this problem and in 1905 General von Schlieffen had come up with a cunning plan.

The Schlieffen Plan

In case of war, the Germans planned to hold off the disorganised Russians in the east (helped by the Austrians), whilst the stronger German forces in the west defeated France.

The Germans knew the French would attack furiously to recover Alsace and Lorraine, but a massive German army planned to surprise the French with a big 'right hook'. They would march behind the French fighting on the border, seize Paris and then march east to catch the French troops in a giant sandwich – War in the West over!

War!

In August 1914 the Schlieffen Plan was put into practice but the 'right hook' involved marching through Belgium, which brought Britain into the War.

The great German attack forced the British, French, and Belgian armies back. As the German armies advanced, their supply lines became stretched and they were forced to swing to the east of Paris. This made it impossible for them to carry out the Schlieffen Plan in full.

As the Germans got near to Paris, General Joffre, the French commander who, however serious the battle was, always stopped for a decent lunch, saw an opportunity to stop them. Rushing all the men he had to the battle front - some reinforcements even came out from Paris by taxi - he pushed the Germans back at the battle of the Marne in September 1914.

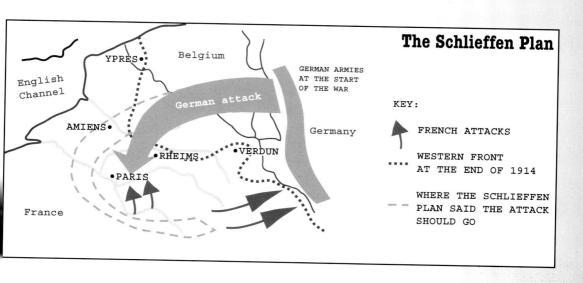

The Schlieffen Plan

English Channel

YPRES

Belgium

GERMAN ARMIES AT THE START OF THE WAR

German attack

Germany

AMIENS

RHEIMS

VERDUN

PARIS

France

KEY:

↑ FRENCH ATTACKS

···· WESTERN FRONT AT THE END OF 1914

– – WHERE THE SCHLIEFFEN PLAN SAID THE ATTACK SHOULD GO

On the Attack!

As Joffre kept on pushing, the French and British armies went on to the attack and by November the Germans were back in Belgium.

In a great battle around the Belgian city of Ypres, the original BEF was pretty much destroyed and the casualties were horrific. The Scots Guards regiment went over to France with about 1000 officers and men; by November 1914 just 1 officer and 69 men were left unwounded.

To escape the shells and bullets the armies 'dug in'; a system of trenches was built from the coast of Belgium through Eastern France to the borders of Switzerland. This became known as the Western Front.

The Christmas Truce

One of the most unusual events of the Great War occurred at Ypres over Christmas 1914. British and German soldiers stopped shooting at each other, climbed out of their trenches, shook hands, wished each other 'a merry Christmas' and exchanged gifts. There was even carol-singing and a football match – but as soon as the generals got to hear about the truce, orders were given that the grim business of killing the enemy, not playing football with him, should continue.

One member of the BEF commented: **"...Scots and Huns were fraternizing in the most genuine possible manner. Every sort of souvenir was exchanged, addresses given and received, photos of families shown etc.....It was absolutely astounding, and if I had seen it on a cinematograph film I would have sworn that it was faked!"**

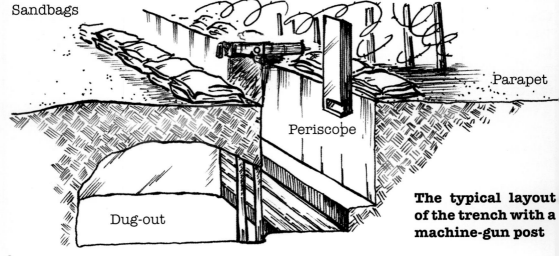

Sandbags

Parapet

Periscope

Dug-out

The typical layout of the trench with a machine-gun post

At the start of the war, two German warships, the 'Goeben' and the 'Breslau', escaped the Royal and French navies in the Mediterranean and arrived in Turkey. This helped to bring Turkey into the War on the German side.

SMS 'Goeben' (www.gwpda.org)

Guernsey seamen were soon in action in distant waters. In the Pacific, the German Admiral Von Spee destroyed a weak Royal Navy squadron at Coronel on the coast of Chile. HMS Good Hope and HMS Monmouth were sunk with all hands. The Admiralty reacted immediately sending HMS Inflexible and HMS Invincible, two powerful battlecruisers, to intercept the German ships in the South Atlantic. In December 1914 these ships defeated Von Spee at the Battle of the Falkland Islands.

Command of the sea meant that the French and British could call up troops from their Empires. German colonies fell rapidly, the one exception being Tanganyika (German East Africa and today's Tanzania) which did not fall until 1918.

British soldiers at Lake Tanganyika (www.firstworldwar.com)

By early 1915 most German merchant shipping had been driven from the seas. The German High Seas Fleet stayed in harbour, reluctant to meet the Royal Navy. However, German submarines (U-boats – 'Untersee Booten') presented an increasing problem.

Guernsey goes to War

The day war broke out...

"We are face to face with the most gigantic struggle that the world has ever seen. Seven European countries, including five Great Powers have drawn the sword........the outcome of the war no man can foretell........ We can only pray that the arms of the Coalition will triumph, that the arrogant 'War Lord' of Germany will be beaten to his knees and that within a short time the forces of the Coalition will meet in Berlin to inaugurate a lasting peace."

Guernsey Weekly Press
Saturday Aug 4th 1914

The Militia

For an island with a population of only about 40,000 people, Guernsey was as well prepared as anywhere in the British Empire when war broke out. As the Island was independent it even had its own defence force – the Militia.

The Militia was made up of two battalions (an army term for a group of about 1000 men), one from 'Town' and the other from the country parishes. There were also gunners and engineers, plus a Cadet Company formed from the boys of Elizabeth College.

In 1914 about 2,000 men were serving in the Militia and its reserves.

Militia training was compulsory for all fit Guernsey men aged between 16 and 60. There were regular evening 'training sessions', an annual camp – held at Les Beaucamps – and a period in the Reserves. Guernsey's part-time soldiers got paid and by 1914 they were as 'highly trained as any peacetime, part-time force could be'.

Guernsey law did not allow the Militia to be sent overseas – other than to rescue the King or to recapture the British mainland from foreign invaders. But it was considered good enough to look after the Island when the regular soldiers from the Garrison at Fort George went to join the fighting in France.

8

Guernsey 'Joins Up'

There was nothing to stop individual Guernsey men volunteering though, and by the end of November 1914 the newspapers reported that 9% of all the men eligible for military service in Guernsey, Alderney and Sark had joined the Army or the Navy – **'a proportion unsurpassed anywhere in the British Isles'**.

Many former soldiers rejoined their regiments. Mr Attewell, originally from Alderney, had nine sons serving in the Army. The youngest Guernseyman to volunteer was Stanley Workman who went to join the Green Howards – a Yorkshire regiment – on his 15th birthday. Fighting families such as these featured frequently in the local papers.

A **Soldier** of the **KING.**

AFTER the War every man who has served will command his Country's gratitude. He will be looked up to and *respected* because he answered his country's call.

The Regiments at the Front are covering themselves with Glory.

Field-Marshal Sir John French wrote in an Order of the day,

"**It is an Honour to belong to such an Army.**"

Every fit man from 19 to 38 is eligible for this great honour. Friends can join in a body, and serve together in the same regiment.

man names
sed some
picion and
son of
nt
cher,
lived
Ierm,
his
er's
mission.

Many of the Frenchmen who had worked in the Islands as farm labourers or domestic servants left to join the French Army, including Jean Rault and the Moreau brothers.

French reservists including Jean Rault from Guernsey (front row right)

"the danger of being killed was small, less than two per cent"

Rev. Colman, speaking at a recruiting meeting in the Forest, stated that "the danger of being killed was small, less than two per cent".

However, the casualties soon mounted up:-

Cecil Francis Crousaz was a regular and a former pupil at Elizabeth College. He was killed in October 1914. His memorial is in Guernsey's Town Church.

Eric d'Auvergne Collings was killed on the Western Front. His memorial is also in the Town Church.

The Moreau brothers were also killed within a day of each other on the Marne in Sept. 1914.

Others included Alfred Solley, Albin Skin, Edmund le Page, Stanley Saunders and Thomas Lihou who died aboard HMS Good Hope, sunk at the Battle of Coronel.

Lieut. Cecil Francis Crousaz
1st South Staffordshire Regiment.

BROTHERS KILLED IN ACTION.

Top: Memorial to Collings

Bottom left :Albin Skin

Guernsey Press obituaries:

Middle: Cecil Crousaz

Bottom right: The Moreau Brothers

In Guernsey life continued much as usual. The Guernsey Press reported the following news items.

Sat 7th Nov 1914 - showing at St Julian's cinema: **Friday, Sat. and Monday Star picture – 'The Tattoo Mark'. Tue. Wed. & Thursday Star picture – 'Blue Pete's Escape' Music by the Santangelo Quartette**

Sat 14th November 1914 - Traffic Accident: **On Saturday afternoon a little girl was knocked down by a motor car in front of Le Riche's Stores, High Street. The driver pulled up with great promptness and the child was picked up unhurt, although she had a very narrow escape from serious injury.**

Saturday 21st November Christmas puddings for the forces (advert): **Make puddings for your soldier friends with ATORA Shredded Beef Suet. They will be more delicious than if made with raw suet. Requires no chopping. Ask your grocer for it!**

Football - Schools League Sat 28th November 1914 Football – Schools League: **Vauvert and St. Sampson's are to meet today at the Cycling Grounds in the Primary Schools' League. Mr. C. Gallis, referee. The kick-off is timed for 2.30. The admission for adults will be twopence and for juniors one penny.**

Guernsey Rabbit and Cavey Show. Saturday December 5th 1914: **The first combined show of rabbits, cavies, cats, poultry and game held under the auspices of the Guernsey Rabbit and Cavy Club opened in the New Market Hall on Wednesday, the venture being crowned with complete success.**

Links with England were disrupted. The steamships which had served the Island were taken for service in the Navy and for those who did sail there was always the risk of meeting a German submarine!

THE GUERNSEY FEATHER AND FUR ASSOCIATION.

A Committee meeting of the above Association was held at Taylor's Restaurant, Commercial Arcade, Wednesday. Mr. J. Carré occupied the chair, in the unavoidable absence of Captain Rawdon McCrea, President.

The business on the agenda was to take into consideration the proposed rules governing the Colonel Bell Memorial Trophies, as drafted at the last meeting. After a few minor alterations they were finally adopted, and now await the approval of the Royal Guernsey Agriucltural and Horticultural Society, whose meeting takes place today.

Before the meeting closed the Secretary was instructed to convey to Mr. E. W. Bachmann, the Committee's deep sympathy with him in his recent sad bereavement.

P. LE PATOUREL
Hon.

Women reading newspapers
Imperial War Museum

Into 1915

On the Western Front, trench warfare settled into a pattern as the British and French armies tried to push the Germans back. There were major battles at Neuve Chapelle, Ypres (again) and along the river Aisne but for little gain and great loss of life. The Germans used poison gas for the first time at Ypres.

Elsewhere in 1915

Things were equally grim on the Eastern Front, the Germans slowly gained the upper hand and the Russians lost millions of men.

The Allies decided to attack Turkey, to try and distract Germany and take the pressure off Russia. It was hoped that the Navy could sail its battleships through a narrow stretch of water, the Dardanelles, and bombard the Turkish capital, Constantinople (now Istanbul) so forcing the Turks to surrender.

This attack failed so soldiers had to be landed at Gallipoli, many of them Australians and New Zealanders, and there was bitter fighting. Nothing was achieved, except 500,000 dead and wounded, and after nine months the Allied forces withdrew leaving Turkey and Germany more strongly allied than before.

Both images: Flanders March 1915 (GMS 1998.6)

German Sniper from Nelson's Picture Weekly 27 Feb 1915

For many people, the Great War means the mud, barbed wire and horror in the trenches of the Western Front.

'Digging in' and creating a system of trenches, with a 'no-man's land' in between, meant that you were always in contact with your enemy. He could never be quite sure when an attack might come and, by being below the surface of the ground, there was less chance of soldiers being killed and wounded in between the big battles.

The British and French saw their trenches as the starting points for attacks as they wanted to push the Germans out of France. Early trenches were built as temporary structures out of sandbags and wood. 'Duckboards' were added to the floor to make walking easier, but in wet weather the trench sometimes became a sea of mud. The Germans stood on the defensive. Their trenches were solidly engineered with deep dugouts often made of concrete. Facing the enemy the trench parapet was built up with sandbags and rolls of barbed wire to stop the other side coming across 'no-man's land'.

By early 1915, about 500 miles (800 kilometres) of trenches had been dug by the opposing armies. They spent the rest of the war trying to break through each others' trenches.

Canadian Troops in Trench (GMAG)

Life on the Front Line

Soldier's Paybook

Most of the time life in the trenches – unless there was a big battle going on – was boring.

Soldiers watched and waited, took care not to get shot by a German marksman from his trench a couple of hundred metres away - cleaned rifles, dug latrines, played cards and wrote home.

Hot food had to come up to the 'front line' trenches from the reserve lines (the rear trenches right at the back of the fighting area), so it was often cold by the time the soldiers got it. Food was usually tinned 'bully' beef (like our corned beef) and vegetables with biscuits and jam. Drinking water was treated with chemicals to make it safe – it tasted awful!

The Germans did not do so well with food as the war progressed as there were terrible shortages in Germany. In fact many of them sent food home to their families!

Lavatories (latrines) were just holes in the ground which smelt dreadful; rats and lice were everywhere. Soldiers generally spent about four days in the 'front line', then eight days in 'reserve' then thirty days away from the Front resting and training. There were always regiments moving up and down to and from 'the Line'. Ordinary (private) soldiers got ten days leave per year and were paid 1 shilling (5p) a day.

Rations (Courtesy Russel Dohe

IWM C02533

Over The Top!

A British soldier going 'over the top' to attack might be carrying as much as 60 lbs (30 kg) of equipment. His basic weapon was his rifle and bayonet but he might also be carrying 'bombs' (hand grenades) or be part of a team carrying a machine gun or a mortar for lobbing grenades at the enemy. He would certainly be carrying his 'entrenching tool' – a spade – and possibly barbed wire or planks of wood to rebuild and defend captured German trenches. Behind the trenches were the artillery lines, the 'guns'. From here massive cannon fired high explosive shells to destroy the enemy's trenches – and his men. Smaller guns fired shrapnel, a shell that burst and flung deadly pieces of metal over the trenches.

Later in the war the guns fired a new horror, shells which burst and covered the trenches with poison gas.

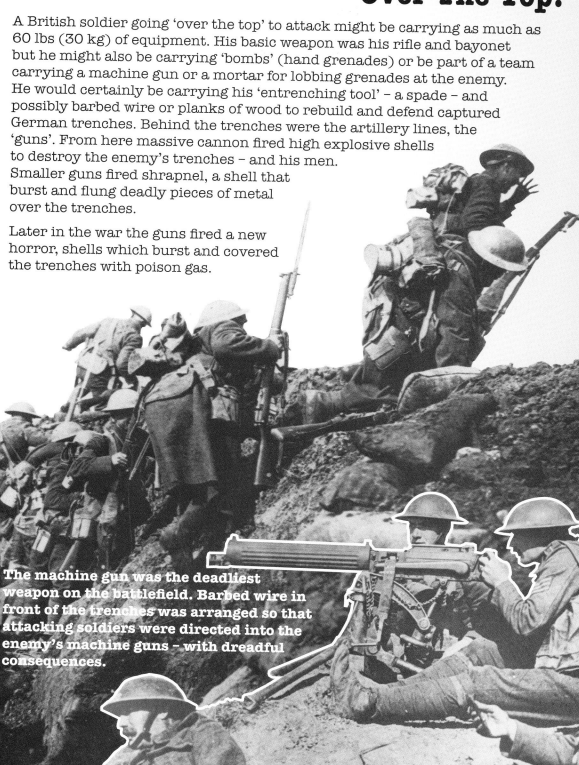

The machine gun was the deadliest weapon on the battlefield. Barbed wire in front of the trenches was arranged so that attacking soldiers were directed into the enemy's machine guns – with dreadful consequences.

The Home Front

Cost of living

By 1915 Guernsey people were beginning to see food prices go up as imports were reduced, ships were lost to enemy submarines and farm workers joined the armed forces. Everything had to come second to the 'war effort'.

Coal, which came to Guernsey from England, was £1 and 8 shillings (£1.40) a ton before the War. By 1918 it was £4 a ton; gas for lighting and heating was made from coal so its price more than doubled too.

By 1917 a Food Control Committee had been set up to distribute food fairly in the Island and a Production Committee, with Jurat Bishop in charge, tried to get the best out of Guernsey farmers. Growers were discouraged from growing flowers and bulbs, potato growers were guaranteed a good price, the export of cattle was banned and fishermen were allowed to fish on Sundays.

	Before the War	By 1918
Big loaf of bread	3p	5p
1lb of Guernsey butter	8p	16p
Pint of Guernsey milk	1p	2p
Pound of tea	6p	11p
Dozen eggs	9p	22p
Pound of cheese	4p	9p

All basic foods increased in price as the list shows (modern money us...

Women had to do men's jobs

Community Kitchen Committee

Guernsey Volunteer Corps

The Guernsey Volunteer Corps

The Guernsey Volunteer Corps was open to 'residents of good character over military age (over 35) but under the physical standard for the army'. They were trained to give military support and often acted as a recruitment unit. This was also seen as a useful way to maintain a feeling of optimism and enthusiasm during the dark days of war. **www.greatwarci.net**

Compulsory rationing

A limited amount of food for each person – meat, sugar and butter was introduced. In Town, the Communal Kitchen, run by Mrs Chepmell Ozanne, the Bailiff's wife, provided hot dinners at cost price and the Schoolchildren's Fund did the same for children all over the Island. Even 'Beanjar' for Sunday breakfast was scarce!

DINNERS FOR SCHOOL CHILDREN

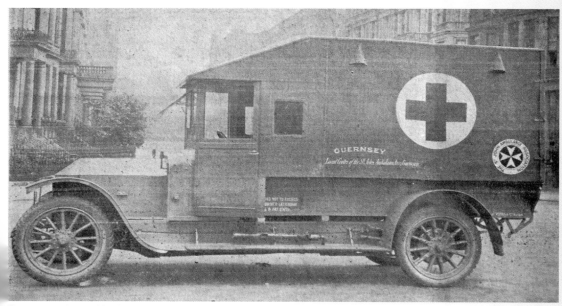

Guernsey people raised funds to provide motor ambulances for the front.

To War!

In March 1915 the States offered to send some of the Guernsey Militia to the Western Front. The men would serve together as companies within existing regiments and as the Royal Irish Regiment and the Royal Irish Fusiliers had been popular garrison regiments in Guernsey before the War, 246 Guernsey officers and men joined these and the artillery.

These Guernseymen, and others sent to replace those killed and wounded, fought at Loos and the Somme in 1916. The heavy casualties at the Somme included the brothers Alfred and Walter Salmon and James Quinn. Private James William Quinn of the 6th Battalion Royal Irish Regiment was killed in action on 15th April 1916 aged 24. He left a widow and two young children.

Private James William Quinn - courtesy of Deputy Francis Quir

Militia to Light Infantry

By 1916 Guernsey was certainly 'doing its bit' for the war effort but the Lieutenant Governor of the day, a crusty old soldier, Lieutenant General Sir Reginald Hart VC, wanted more. He felt that a regiment with the name 'Guernsey' should be in action on the Western Front and he persuaded the States to introduce conscription (compulsory military service for men of the right age) and to offer the Militia to the War Office in London as a 'service battalion'. On December 17th 1916 the Militia was suspended and the Royal Guernsey Light Infantry (RGLI) came into being.

Lieutenant General Sir Reginald Hart VC
Courtesy of Government House

RGLI 'On Parade' (GMAG RGLI BJ 118a)

The Battle of the Somme

In February 1916 the Germans attacked the French at Verdun. To help divert German forces the British launched a massive attack on the German defences overlooking the River Somme in July 1916. The British guns shelled the German lines for a week and great mines were exploded under some of the German trenches. However, much of the German barbed wire remained uncut and many of the deep German dugouts were unharmed. As the British troops went 'over the top' and walked in long lines towards the German trenches, the German machine-gunners raced up from their dug-outs, manned their guns and opened fire. The result was a massacre, the British lost 20,000 men killed and 40,000 wounded in the first hour of the battle.

The battle dragged on until November with the weather turning wetter and wetter. Repeated attacks became bogged down in the mud. At the end, the British Army had lost about 420,000 men, killed and wounded. They had advanced 7 miles. German casualties matched those of the British.

The battle at Verdun had also achieved little – except the loss of one million men.

These battles were typical of the futility of much of the fighting on the Western Front.

British Tommies rescuing a comrade under shell fire. (IWM Q79501)

The Somme (IWM Q042233)

Royal Guernsey Light Infantry

Guernsey was very proud of its new regiment. Officers came back from the Irish regiments to join up and a group of Guernsey quarrymen formed a company in the Royal Engineers.

Further training took place at L'Ancresse, Les Beaucamps and Fort George and on June 1st 1917 the RGLI set off for England.

RGLI in Training (GMAG RGLI BJ 30 and 31)

RGLI on route march near Canterbury (GMAG RGLI BJ)

Once in England there was more training and by October 1917 they were on their way to the Western Front at Ypres in Belgium.

In training at Fort George, Guernsey (GMAG BJ 162a)

The Royal Guernsey Light Infantry

From there the Guernseymen went to a training camp at Arras in France before the next big battle, at Cambrai, in November 1917.

Colours being presented to the RGLI May 1917 (GMAG RGLI 48)

Light Infantry?

In the days of Napoleon and the Duke of Wellington foot soldiers or infantrymen, came in two sorts. The infantry 'of the line' stood in solid ranks and fired their muskets at each other at close range. The 'light' infantry fought in much looser style and fired at the enemy from behind trees and humps. By the time the Royal Guernsey Light Infantry got involved in the War, the Western Front had made the distinction which their title suggested out of date.

RGLI soldiers with 'Joey' the RGLI Mascot. (GMAG RGLI55)

Ada's Story - Part 1

When war broke out, Ada Le Poidevin was a single, nineteen year old girl, whose family lived in Dorey's Cottages, in Nocq Road St Sampson's.

The Le Poidevin sisters, like many young women of that era, were in domestic service; Alice working as a cook and Ada as a parlour maid. However soon after the start of the war, the Victoria Cottage Hospital at Amherst became a Class A military hospital, and Ada went to work there in 1915/16. Then in April 1917, not long after conscription had come into force in the island, she responded to an advertisement in the Salvation Army publication the War Cry for "Twenty-five women Salvationists to assist in our Refreshment and Recreation huts with the Troops in France".

Ada Le Poidevin in her Salvation Army uniform, April 1917

She came from an ordinary working class background – her father, John Wesley Le Poidevin was a carter in a local quarry and her mother, Alice was a midwife. The family were ardent Salvationists, attending the Nocq Road Citadel. Ada's father and brother were in the band, and both parents were involved with the Sunday school while she and her sister Alice were Songsters.

Inside a typical Salvation Army Rest Hut

The fact that she volunteered may have been because her father was too old to be called up, her only brother was too young, while her sister was by this time married with a baby, so she would have been the only family member able to 'do her bit'.

Learn more about Ada at **www.adaswar.net**

Women to the fore!

When the men marched away the women of Guernsey – and the rest of Britain – stepped forward to take their places and were soon doing all manner of tasks that ten years earlier would have been thought impossible for a woman. Many went because they had lost a husband, son or brother to the war.

In shops, offices and banks women took easily to 'men's work'. Soon female insurance agents, newspaper reporters and Post Office messengers were a common sight in the streets of St. Peter Port.

By 1917 Miss Agnes Sebire (L'Ancresse), Miss Dylis Richards (Pike's Corner), Miss Huxford (Red Lion) and Mrs. Mitchell (L'Islet) were all working as 'conductorettes' on the trams of the Guernsey Railway Company running between Town and The Bridge. Later that year Miss Sebire became a driver.

In March 1917 Mr. Gilroy, a grower at Pleinheaume, advertised for more men. He had no replies but did receive 37 applications from women. In the end he employed just two, Miss Laura Le Page and Miss Elsie Sebire, but he paid them a fraction of what he paid his men! Nonetheless women working in the vineries and on the farms became a common sight.

Local hospitals like the Victoria Cottage Hospital at Amherst and Les Touillets in the Castel became military hospitals. Some nurses went overseas; Miss Galliott of St. Martin's serving with the Queen Alexandra Imperial Military Nursing Service, finished up at Salonika in Greece.

Nurse Galliott

Some women went to England to be involved in war work. Factories making shells and bombs were dangerous and unhealthy places. Mrs. Knight of St. Martin's and the Coutu sisters of St. Peter Port 'did their bit' whilst Mrs. Sackett of St. Peter Port and Mrs. Coe of St. Andrew's worked in Manchester making clothes for wounded soldiers.

THE EXIGENCIES OF WAR

MUNITION WORKERS.

A WAR WORKER.

The War at Sea

The Royal Navy was the country's pride and joy, so it was expected to meet the German Fleet and send it rapidly to the bottom of the North Sea.

The Germans did not like that idea at all. They kept the battleships of their High Seas Fleet in harbour, only coming out if they thought the coast was clear. The Royal Navy battleships, the Grand Fleet, were tied up watching and waiting so the war at sea was about smaller ships, blockades and submarines. Three sailors with a Guernsey connection illustrate this very well.

Rear Admiral Osmond de Beauvoir Brock

Rear Admiral Osmond de Beauvoir Brock was a son of the famous Guernsey family, although he did not actually live in the Island. He served in the Grand Fleet.

On January 24th 1915 Captain Brock, as he was then, was in command of the battlecruiser HMS 'Princess Royal'

Rear Admiral Osmond de Beauvoir Brock (top centre)

at the Battle of the Dogger Bank. The Royal Navy won the battle but poor signalling let all but one of the German ships escape. However, Brock was promoted after the battle and on May 31st 1916 he was the admiral in command of the First Battlecruiser Squadron, HMS 'Princess Royal', HMS 'Queen Mary' and HMS 'Tiger' at the Battle of Jutland.

Jutland was the only battle in the entire war when the Grand Fleet met the German High Seas Fleet. The Royal Navy suffered heavy losses but trapped the German fleet which had to make a rapid escape back to port where it stayed for the rest of the war, leaving the Royal Navy in control of the seas. An American journalist said of the battle 'the German fleet has assaulted its jailer but it is now safely back in jail'.

Rear Admiral Brock was present when the German fleet sailed into the Firth of Forth to surrender on November 21st 1918.

H.M.S. Princess Royal.

Vice Admiral Sir Reginald Tupper

Vice Admiral Sir Reginald Tupper was from a renowned Guernsey seafaring family. For much of the war he commanded the 10th Cruiser Squadron and his flagship was the 'Alsatian'. 'Alsatian' was not a proper warship; she was an armed merchant cruiser (i.e. a pre-war liner fitted with a few small guns and pressed into naval service).

Admiral Tupper's squadron of about twenty ships like 'Alsatian' and twenty armed trawlers, patrolled the stormy waters of the North Atlantic between Scotland and Iceland. They were not meant to fight German warships; their duty was to enforce the Blockade. They stopped and searched neutral ships and if those ships were carrying anything that could be useful to Germany in fighting the war such as food, raw materials or weapons, it was arrested and sent to a British port. It was a tedious and dangerous duty but the 10th Cruiser Squadron stopped and searched about 15,000 ships during the War. Slowly Germany ran out of supplies with which to fight and the Admiralty complimented Admiral Tupper on 'the magnificent work of the Blockade which had crushed the life out of the Central Powers'.

You can see Admiral Tupper's memorial and his flag from the 'Alsatian' on display in Guernsey's Town Church

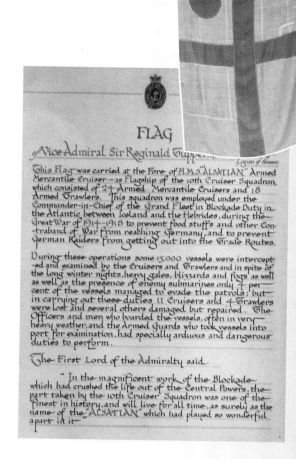

FLAG

of Vice Admiral Sir Reginald Tupper.

This Flag was carried at the Fore of H.M.S. 'ALSATIAN' Armed Mercantile Cruiser – as Flagship of the 10th Cruiser Squadron, which consisted of 24 Armed Mercantile Cruisers and 18 Armed Trawlers. This squadron was employed under the Commander-in-Chief of the Grand Fleet in Blockade Duty in the Atlantic between Iceland and the Hebrides, during the Great War of 1914-1918 to prevent food stuffs and other contraband of War from reaching Germany, and to prevent German Raiders from getting out into the Trade Routes.

During these operations some 15,000 vessels were intercepted and examined by the Cruisers and Trawlers and in spite of the long winter nights, heavy gales, blizzards and fogs as well as the presence of enemy submarines only 4 per cent of the vessels managed to evade the patrols; but in carrying out these duties 11 Cruisers and 4 Trawlers were lost and several others damaged but repaired. The Officers and men who boarded the vessels, often in very heavy weather, and the Armed Guards who took vessels into port for examination, had specially arduous and dangerous duties to perform.

The First Lord of the Admiralty said

"In the magnificent work of the Blockade which had crushed the life out of the Central Powers, the part taken by the 10th Cruiser Squadron was one of the finest in history, and will live for all time, as surely as the name of the 'ALSATIAN' which had played so wonderful a part in it"

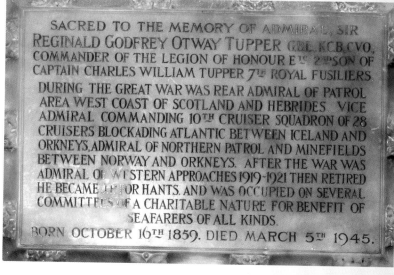

SACRED TO THE MEMORY OF ADMIRAL SIR REGINALD GODFREY OTWAY TUPPER GBE, KCB, CVO, COMMANDER OF THE LEGION OF HONOUR E 2ND SON OF CAPTAIN CHARLES WILLIAM TUPPER 7TH ROYAL FUSILIERS DURING THE GREAT WAR WAS REAR ADMIRAL OF PATROL AREA WEST COAST OF SCOTLAND AND HEBRIDES VICE ADMIRAL COMMANDING 10TH CRUISER SQUADRON OF 28 CRUISERS BLOCKADING ATLANTIC BETWEEN ICELAND AND ORKNEYS, ADMIRAL OF NORTHERN PATROL AND MINEFIELDS BETWEEN NORWAY AND ORKNEYS. AFTER THE WAR WAS ADMIRAL OF WESTERN APPROACHES 1919-1921 THEN RETIRED HE BECAME J.P. FOR HANTS. AND WAS OCCUPIED ON SEVERAL COMMITTEES OF A CHARITABLE NATURE FOR BENEFIT OF SEAFARERS OF ALL KINDS. BORN OCTOBER 16TH 1859. DIED MARCH 5TH 1945.

Able Seaman John Helman

Able Seaman John Helman joined the Navy as a Boy Seaman in 1913 when he was 17. His family had moved to Guernsey in about 1900 and they lived at Trent Cottages, Castel Hill.

In February 1918 Able Seaman Helman volunteered for 'special duties' which turned out to be an attack on Zeebrugge on the Belgian Coast. Zeebrugge was a base for German U-boats which were sinking many British ships. On April 23rd 1918 two old cruisers were sunk in the mouth of the harbour to block the waterway and two ferries carried troops to attack the German defences. A fierce battle took place and many lives were lost but it only took about a week before the U-boats were using Zeebrugge again.

Able Seaman Helman was wounded in the attack. He spent some time in the Navy hospital at Plymouth before coming back to Guernsey in 1919 with a pension of £2 per week. He died in February 1920, aged only 23.

Able Seaman John Helman

John Helman's memorial in St Andrew's churchyard

Wars always lead to new inventions, even if those inventions are only more efficient ways of killing people and destroying things.

Submarines

German submarines were always referred to as U-boats.

Submarines had to operate by certain rules: enemy warships could be attacked without warning but merchant ships had to be checked to find out if they belonged to an enemy country or were neutral before they could be sunk.

On May 27th 1917 the sailing ship 'Mary Anne' from Fowey in Cornwall was off the west coast of Guernsey when a U-Boat surfaced alongside her. The crew were allowed to get into their lifeboat and row over to Guernsey, but the submarine's crew put explosives in the 'Mary Anne' and left her to sink. 'Mary Anne' (being a tough old ship) did not sink but was found later drifting off Sark so she was towed into St. Peter Port and repaired.

Once on the surface a submarine was not such a deadly weapon; the railway steamship 'Ibex', sailing from Weymouth to Guernsey actually sank a U-boat and the crew received a £500 prize.

However, some German submarine captains fired their torpedoes first and asked questions afterwards. This became known as 'unrestricted submarine warfare' and in 1916 and 1917 it nearly defeated Britain. Fortunately, the Royal Navy remembered the 'convoy' system and soon all merchant ships sailed in groups protected by warships and airships. It became much harder for the U-boats to sink merchant ships. However, 'unrestricted submarine warfare' brought America into the War on the side of Britain and France.

The end of the Mary Anne June 1917 (GMAG RGLI bJ 107)

German Submarine (IWM Q20220)

Airships

One of the museums in Castle Cornet in Guernsey tells the story of the 201 Squadron of the Royal Air Force, 'Guernsey's Own'. But 201 Squadron started out during the Great War as No.1 Squadron, Royal Naval Air Service and its first squadron hero was Rex Warneford. Flight Sub-Lieutenant Warneford was the first man to shoot down a 'Zeppelin'.

In Germany, before the Great War, Count Ferdinand von Zeppelin had developed 'airships'. His Zeppelins, as they were called, were rigid, cigar-shaped balloons full of hydrogen, a gas which is lighter than air. The engines and a 'gondola' for the airship crew and passengers were suspended below. In calm conditions the Zeppelins, which were up to 170 metres long, were safe and reliable and for a few years operated a passenger service all over Germany.

With the outbreak of war Zeppelins were used as 'scouts' for the German fleet and to bomb English cities, thus becoming the latest terror weapon.

Zeppelins flew slowly but too high for the aeroplanes of the day to attack them, so when Rex Warneford shot down Zeppelin LZ37 over Belgium it was a great triumph and he was awarded the Victoria Cross. However, Zeppelins, full of inflammable hydrogen, caught fire very easily and eventually smaller and faster airships called 'blimps' were developed instead.

Aeroplanes

Flight Sub Lieutenant Rex Warneford

In 1914 the few aeroplanes around were just rich men's toys but by 1918 aeroplanes were being used by both sides to bomb each other's cities. Over the Western Front 'aces' in colourful biplanes fought each other to control the sky. The most famous 'ace' was the German, Manfred von Richthofen, 'The Red Baron'. He is thought to have shot down about 80 British and French aircraft.

Guernsey's Seaplane base

Guernsey people became used to aeroplanes in 1917 when a French seaplane base was set up on the Castle Emplacement. The Model Yacht Pond was drained to provide the site for one of four hangars and buildings were constructed as living accommodation and stores. The seaplanes themselves were moored in the harbour and taxied out beyond the lighthouse to take off.

French seaplanes in St Peter Port Harbour (GMAG)

If they needed to come out of the water for repair they were lifted using a crane.

The base usually had up to 12 seaplanes at any one time and had two main duties: locating and destroying German U-boats which were attacking shipping around the Channel Islands, and escorting convoys travelling from the coast of Brittany past Guernsey and Alderney and on towards Cherbourg.

A French Seaplane off Sark (GMAG GLI BJ 120a)

Seaplanes from Guernsey carried out 25 attacks on submarines and discovered three newly laid minefields designed to disrupt shipping.

At the end of the War the French authorities awarded the base the Croix de Guerre – a medal for outstanding service.

Building the hangar for the seaplanes over the Model Yacht Pond

Tanks

On land something was needed to overcome the deadlock of barbed wire, machine guns and trenches on the Western Front. So a 'mechanised armoured fighting vehicle' was developed. To confuse the Germans the British pretended that the new vehicles were to carry water – so they were called 'tanks'!

The first tanks weighed 27 tons and were armed with machine guns and small cannon. They had caterpillar tracks to enable them to cross trenches and ditches and travelled at about 4 miles an hour over level ground.

Though noisy and dangerous to drive into action, they could crush barbed wire and their steel plating kept out machine gun bullets. On seeing tanks for the first time German soldiers cried 'The Devil is coming'.

A few tanks were used in the later stages of the Battle of the Somme but the first mass use of tanks was at the Battle of Cambrai in November 1917 – a battle in which the Royal Guernsey Light Infantry got its first real taste of action.

Often tanks got stuck! (IWM Q6432)

The Battle of Cambrai

November - December 1917

The Royal Guernsey Light Infantry (RGLI) first went into battle at Cambrai in Northern France on November 20th 1917. The newly-formed Tank Corps proposed a large scale raid on the German trenches to prove what tanks could do. The raid turned into a full-scale attack on part of the Hindenburg Line, one of the strongest parts of the German front line, near the town of Cambrai.

Private Latimer Thomas Le Poidevin of the RGLI wrote up his wartime experiences in a journal:

656 Private Latimer Thomas Le Poidevin, 1st (Service) Battalion, RGLI

'while on active service from the time I joined up to the time I got demobilised'.

At 0620 hrs. on November 20th 1917, behind an intense bombardment provided by 1000 guns, 376 tanks led by the commander of the Tank Corps, General Elles, in the tank 'Hilda', crossed the British front line and headed for the German trenches.

They were supported by 275 aircraft of the Royal Flying Corps and 6 divisions (about 70,000 men) of infantry – including the RGLI.

'Then an hour before day break the barrage started. My word, it was just a mass of fire lifting from the earth and the working of those tanks coming out from their hiding places. Then it was our turn to go over the top but we stopped between the old front line of ours and the enemy...with two tanks working with us we began to attack our objective which *was Number Nine Wood and casualties was small up to this time.*

The mass of tanks terrified the German soldiers who began to surrender. With a few hold-ups the attack went on until, by midday, 2000 Germans were prisoners, a 6 mile section of the Hindenburg Line had been captured and British troops and tanks had advanced nearly 3 miles. A great victory was in prospect, all that now remained was for the reinforcements to come up and overcome a few pockets of stubborn German resistance and then the cavalry could gallop through and capture Cambrai.

But it never happened, orders got confused and the advance slowed down. Now the British troops formed a 'salient' – pushing into German territory but capable of being counter-attacked on three sides. The Germans were very good at counter-attacks.

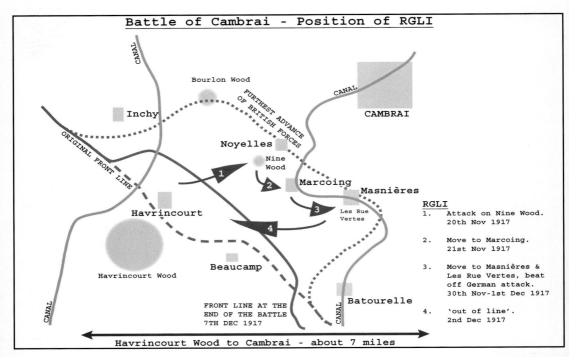

Battle of Cambrai - Position of RGLI

CANAL

Bourlon Wood

Inchy

CANAL

CAMBRAI

FURTHEST ADVANCE OF BRITISH FORCES

ORIGINAL FRONT LINE

Noyelles

Nine Wood

1

2

Marcoing

Masnières

Havrincourt

3

Les Rue Vertes

4

Beaucamp

Havrincourt Wood

CANAL

FRONT LINE AT THE END OF THE BATTLE 7TH DEC 1917

CANAL

Batourelle

RGLI
1. Attack on Nine Wood. 20th Nov 1917

2. Move to Marcoing. 21st Nov 1917

3. Move to Masnières & Les Rue Vertes, beat off German attack. 30th Nov-1st Dec 1917

4. 'out of line'. 2nd Dec 1917

Havrincourt Wood to Cambrai - about 7 miles

'Early next morning we had a small counter-attack...We could see some people coming towards us with long coats and it seemed as if it was women carrying their babies in their arms, but instead it was old Jerry with their machine guns and they opened fire on us'.

Later that day (November 21st) the RGLI moved south a mile or so to the village of Marcoing.

'Our company got billeted on a French farm...We were in this place for a 48 hour rest, although we could hear the noise of shells coming from Jerry and exploding in the village, wondering if they would hit this place'.

On the afternoon of November 25th the RGLI went back into the front line at the small town of Masnières.

'One shell pitched right into our trench, killing six of the boys and wounded many. Then, when things became quiet, they asked for men to carry the dead and wounded down by a canal, so I was helping with the first lot...We spent 5 days in these trenches'.

On November 26th Private Le Poidevin's brother, Lance-Corporal Herbert John Le Poidevin was killed in action.

'So what I done I went and found A Company and saw his section commander, so I was told of how he met his death'

On November 30th the RGLI took up a defensive position at Les Rues Vertes (part of Masnières) and withstood a desperate German attack which included poison gas shells. **'Everyman, signallers, cooks, officer's servants and clerks turned out and joined in the battle'.**

'a Lewis gun team was wanted on his left flank....we was sent and it was so dangerous as we had to go over one of these bridges....On this side of the canal the ground was low and wet with very tall grass growing....We stayed in this muddy place until night before being able to stand up or walk about...and about midnight when an Officer visited us we reminded him that we hadn't seen food yet that day'.

General Haig, commanding the British Army, noted that **'on the Masnières front the 29th Division, composed of English, Scottish, Welsh, Irish, Guernsey and Newfoundland battalions...most gallantly beat off a succession of powerful assaults and maintained their line intact'.**

'About midnight on Dec. 1st 1917 we were told that the Division was getting relieved. This evening it was lovely moonlight...As we passed by the bridge three of our gun team was put to watch the bridge, me being on...as a rearguard for the battalion...it was an unpleasant job, as our gun was out of action, so while two men was trying to put it together that left me to watch with my rifle, and not a soul was to be heard.

At about 2 o'clock in the morning of Dec. 2nd our Officer came back and ordered us to pack up, and follow him as we was leaving the village altogether. My word we walked with a light foot, although not having had any food for two days and close on two weeks that we hadn't shaved or had a good wash... When daylight arrived we had our rations given for the day, so we made the best of them for our breakfast'.

By December 3rd the battle was over, the German attacks had ceased and for all the great courage and bloodshed – and the initial success of the tanks – the front lines were still pretty much in the same places as they had been when the battle started.

On December 4th 'we arrived at Fins, the village where we started from for the battle...........the boys looked rough, but after having a shave and wash we began to look as A1'

Private Le Poidevin's optimistic mood must have been stretched to the limit over the next few days as the losses suffered by the RGLI became apparent.

But at what cost?

After the battle the Commanding Officer of the 29th Division, of which the RGLI was a part wrote to the Bailiff: 'I want to convey to the Guernsey Authorities my very high appreciation of the valuable services rendered by the Royal Guernsey Light Infantry in the Battle of Cambrai. It was a wonderful effort.........Guernsey has every reason to feel the greatest pride in her sons and I am proud to have them fighting alongside my staunch veterans of three years fighting experience'.

The RGLI went into the battle with about 1200 officers and men.

On December 3rd Private Le Poidevin noted:

'after roll call the Battalion was left with 501 men'.

The official casualty figures indicate over 120 killed, 85 on December 1st alone, with more dying later from wounds received in the battle. About 250 received wounds from which they recovered and a further 250 or so were listed as missing, that is they were wounded, gassed or taken prisoner.

Cambrai memorial at Louverval (detail)

Private John Henry from Vazon served in the RGLI. He was wounded and taken prisoner on December 1st 1917 during the Battle of Cambrai.

Of his time in captivity he said:-

'I was taken to a hospital at Le Cateau and my wounds were dressed at once'

'A German doctor, Dr. Ellerbeck, attended me (at another hospital). He was a good doctor and he saw that my wounds were dressed everyday.......but they had to use paper bandages'

'The food here was quite eatable but I could have done with more consistency'

'I received Red Cross parcels, but some had articles removed, usually either soap, tea, sugar or cigarettes'

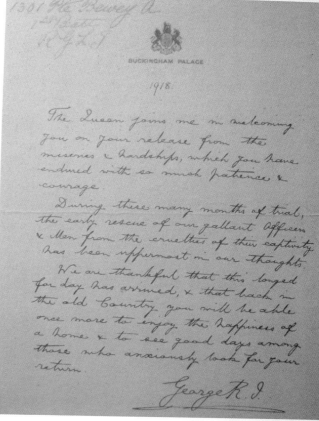

Letter from King George V sent to 1301 Private Albert Bewey on his release. Courtesy of Jansen Bewey.

'The treatment of prisoners I consider to have been very fair and I never saw any cruelty........the (German) people looked pretty hungry'

Private Henry was sent back to England through Holland and was back in London by September 1918.

Postcard sent to 1511 Private Albert Edward Le Huray while he was a Prisoner of War in Prussia.

Casualties

Wounded men were passed back to Casualty Clearing Stations where doctors could treat them.

A 'Blighty one' was a wound which did not kill you but which got you home to England and out of the war without too serious an injury.

'Trench foot' was a common complaint caused by standing about in the mud and damp of the trenches.

'Shell shock' came to be recognised as a state of mind brought on by the horror and noise of the trenches – but not before some soldiers had been found guilty of cowardice and shot, through no fault of their own.

Guernseyman Private Parry convalescing among friends (GMAG)

First Aid Post in France (GMAG)

If a soldier was killed in battle his friends tried to bury him where he had fallen. But in some places the ground was fought over many times and these bodies were churned up and lost in the mess of battle.

Later, when the war had ended, peaceful cemeteries across Eastern France and Belgium with row upon row of white headstones were built to commemorate the fallen. These still mark where the Front had been.

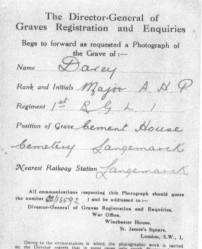

The Director-General of Graves Registration and Enquiries

Begs to forward as requested a Photograph of the Grave of :—

Name *Davey*

Rank and Initials *Major A. H. P.*

Regiment *1st R G L 1*

Position of Grave *Cement House Cemetery Langemarck*

Nearest Railway Station *Langemarck*

All communications respecting this Photograph should quote the number 82/3592) and be addressed to :—
Director-General of Graves Registration and Enquiries,
War Office,
Winchester House,
St. James's Square,
London, S.W., 1.

Owing to the circumstances in which the photographic work is carried on, the Director regrets that in some cases only rough Photographs can be obtained.

"COPYRIGHT FULLY RESERVED."

Graves that did survive were marked with a wooden cross

Official letter sent to Mrs Davey confirming where her husband was buried

Faubourg d'Amiens Cemetery in a busy part of the town of Arras. www.greatwarci.net

Also in 1916 & 1917

In April 1916, a combined British and Indian army surrendered to the Turks in Iraq. By late 1917 the British advanced to capture Baghdad and Jerusalem.

Richard de Beauvoir de Lisle of the Indian Army was killed in Mesopotamia in 1916. His memorial is in Guernsey's Town Church.

On the Eastern Front Germany gained the upper hand and, as Russian casualties grew, unrest deepened in Russia. This resulted in a number of revolutions which deposed the Emperor (Tsar) and took Russia out of the War.

On April 6th 1917 America, exasperated by the Germans' unrestricted submarine warfare and alarmed that Germany might help Mexico to invade the south western states of the USA, declared war on Germany.

de Lisle's Memorial in Guernsey's 'Town Church'

On the Western Front the British launched a major attack at Passchendaele. By November the British had advanced 800 yards and lost 250,000 men. German casualties were nearer 300,000.

Passchendaele 31 July 1917 (IWM E(AU

Ada's story - Part 2

Ada went to England in April 1917 and helped to man one of the Salvation Army huts on Salisbury Plain. These huts provided the soldiers with 'home comforts', tea and decent food and a chance to relax for an hour or two away from the War – or more training in the case of Salisbury Plain. By autumn 1917 Ada was in France where she continued working in Salvation Rest Huts at Ostrohove and Abbeville.

Of the battlefields she said 'nothing but ruins to see' and she was under fire a number of times.

'Slept in barn. Jerry over. Dropped five around us. Shrapnel through roof. Awful experience'

Some Salvation Army hostels were on the roads where the soldiers marched up and down to the Front. The young 'sisters' provided tea and, where possible, home cooked food. Mrs Huish at Etaples - one of the biggest camps - is supposed to have fried 2,000 eggs in a day!

The 'sisters' washed and mended men's uniforms, and also simply sat and talked to the soldiers, taking their minds off the War. Religious meetings were also provided for those who might find comfort from them. There was never any scandal and General Haig thought it good for the morale of the soldiers to have Salvation Army women like Ada so close to the front line.

Ada seated 3rd from left outside a Salvation Army hut 'Somewhere in France'

1918 - the Death of a Regiment

Germany was in trouble. Although Russia was out of the War, more and more American soldiers were joining the Allied armies on the Western Front.

In Germany, food and raw materials were in short supply – a result of the Royal Navy's blockade – and there were strikes by workers in Berlin. The High Seas Fleet was near mutiny.

The German generals tried one last throw. In March they launched 'the Kaiser's battle' and began to drive the Allies back. General Haig was near to panic, **'With our backs to the wall and believing in the justice of our cause, each one of us must fight on to the end'**.

THE RGLI

In January 1918 the Royal Guernsey Light Infantry (RGLI) was in the front line at Passchaendaele, near Ypres in Belgium. Many of the men killed or wounded at Cambrai had been replaced by others who were not from the Island.

They were not involved in a big battle but there was still a steady trickle of casualties from daily shelling and shooting. Private Le Poidevin commented **'this part was a very lonely and rough place'**.

With the big German attacks the RGLI was moved south into France near the town of Hazebrouck to help defend the important railway junctions there. There was fierce fighting and the RGLI took terrible casualties. When the fighting died down and the survivors regrouped, Private Le Poidevin said there **'was 55 men and two officers'** left. The RGLI had marched into battle with 483 men and 20 officers.

It was the death of the regiment.

For the rest of the war the RGLI, with too few men to make a proper fighting force, provided the guard for General Haig's headquarters at Montreuil.

RGLI on parade at Montreuil (GMAG RGLI BJ)

The End of Hostilities

The German attack eventually ran out of steam – and more importantly, reinforcements and supplies. The Allies counter-attacked and by October everyone was back were they had started in 1914.

On November 11th 1918 an Armistice (truce) was agreed and the guns fell silent. However, it wasn't until May 1919 that a formal peace treaty was signed at Versailles, near Paris.

The Allies had won.

The Allies imposed very hard terms on Germany, who they held to be completely responsible for the War. So hard were these terms and so badly did many Germans feel about the way they were treated that the Treaty of Versailles may have contributed to the outbreak of the Second World War twenty years later.

RGLI troops return to Guernsey 22 May 1919 (GMAG RGLI 241)

To our Comrades in Arms who formed the
1st. (Service) Battalion
Royal Guernsey Light Infantry.

The time has now arrived when we are to be demobilised, when we can lay aside our weapons of offense and once again resume our peaceful avocations.

May I express to you on behalf of all Officers our heartfelt thanks and great appreciation for the loyal support you have given to us on all occasions.

You have shown that troops strong in *morale* and *esprit-de-corps* will in an emergency rise superior to their opponents, and acquit themselves with credit—(Cambrai, 1917).

Whether it was during those long periods of holding the shell-hole area in the Paaschendale Salient, or the operations of the Battle of the Lys, or through those anxious times of the enemy's great offensive, March-July, 1918, you have never failed to maintain by your conduct, the traditions of your forefathers.

It has been your privilege to furnish guards at the "Chateau" of the Commander-in-Chief as well as at General Headquarters, and to do honour to the Commanders of the Allied Armies.

We earnestly hope that as the years go by we shall be able to keep in touch with each other; we shall stand together in the future as we have done in the past, and should occasion arise, hold out the right hand of friendship to those who need it.

I wish, on behalf of all Officers, everyone now in the Battalion, or who has been in it, success and happiness in whatever he may undertake.

A la prochaine,

T. L. de Havilland

Lieut.-Colonel,
Commanding 1st (S) Bn. Royal Guernsey Light Infantry.
France, May, 1919.

To _____

BANKS, BROWNSEY & CO., GUERNSEY.

Coming home

When the War was over, the Prime Minister of Britain promised that the soldiers would come back to 'a land fit for heroes', but Guernsey, like so many other places had a lot to cope with.

In May 1919 the survivors of the Royal Guernsey Light Infantry sailed home to Guernsey on the SS 'Lydia', one of the railway steamships that had served the Island before the War. They found a Guernsey much changed.

There had been food shortages as U-boats had threatened the ships bringing in supplies. Farms and vineries had suffered without the young men who had gone to war and links with France had almost disappeared.

An outbreak of Spanish flu killed a number of women and children just before the men came home.

RGLI return to Guernsey 22 May 1919 (GMAG)

The women (who traditionally only worked in the home) had taken on the men's work and with no markets to send produce to – or tourists – there was less work for the returning troops.

The stress and strain on local people was reflected in newspaper stories of robbery, drunkenness, child neglect and violence. Maybe it was not a coincidence that Guernsey's first regular police force dates from 1919.

To create employment the States invested in 'job creation' projects such as the building of the magnificent cliff paths along the South Coast. The Guernsey tomato and flower industries were re-organised and slowly the tourists came back. A few came on the new seaplane service started in 1923.

Building South Coast paths

Guernsey's 'Lost Generation'

There was also the 'Lost Generation' of men who did not return. In a small island like Guernsey their loss made a large hole in the population and affected virtually every family.

	Went to fight	Killed in action
Guernsey	5109	1112
Alderney	116	43
Sark	48	17
Totals	**5273**	**1172**

1 in 5 of those who marched away from the Bailiwick did not come back; in Sark it was 1 in 3, a terrible effect on a remote island community.

The War Memorial at the top of Smith Street in St Peter Port shows:

13 - Le Pages, 12 - Fallas, 10 - Tostevins, 9 - Ozannes, 8 - Ogiers, 8 - Duquemins ..... the list goes on.

Most of those with a traditional Guernsey surname will find someone from their family on that memorial. Parishes also had memorials though some have been moved - such as the St Peter Port one which is now in a local supermarket.

The census figures show what a terrible effect the War had on the population:

	Men	Women	Total
1911	20661	21197	41858
1921	18246	20069	38315

Some men came home but were affected by the horrors they had experienced. Others died of their injuries – Able Seaman Helman has already been mentioned, Frank de Mouilpied Laine of the RGLI, who died in 1922, is also buried in St Andrew's churchyard.

It was not until the mid-1930s that the population of Guernsey, Alderney and Sark grew back to the level it had been before the War.

The War had cost the British government so much, that the States of Guernsey were invited to make a contribution. They paid over £300,000 in total - equivalent to six million pounds today.

The Poppy came to symbolise the fallen.

Decorations and Awards

Many Guerneymen received awards for gallantry. Those listed below are only a small selection. See **www.greatwarci.net** for more information.

The highest award for bravery was the Victoria Cross (VC). The highest for 'distinguished conduct in the field' was the Distinguished Conduct Medal (DCM). The Military Cross (MC), introduced in 1914, was awarded to 'junior' Officers and 'senior' other ranks. The Military Medal (MM), introduced in 1916, was awarded to other ranks.

THE DISTINGUISHED CONDUCT MEDAL

569 Acting Sergeant Walter Herbert Budden 1st (Service) Battalion RGLI

590 Sergeant William J Le Poidevin 1st (Service) Battalion RGLI

Medals awarded to Sergeant W J Le Poidevin

MILITARY CROSS

Temporary Captain Herbert Arthur Le Bas 1st (Service) Battalion, RGLI

Lieutenant Edgar James Stone 1st (Service) Battalion, RGLI

Lieutenant Harry Easterbrook Knollys Stranger 1st (Service) Battalion, RGLI

MILITARY MEDAL

843 Corporal Joseph Sealley 1st (Service) Battalion, RGLI

841 Private Thomas R. Robins 1st (Service) Battalion, RGLI

610 Private Cecil H. Yeagers 1st (Service) Battalion, RGLI

Ada's story - Part 3

When the War ended Ada and some of her Salvation Army 'sisters' became involved with the Salvation Army War Graves Visitation Department. They met parties of people who had lost relatives on the Western Front and escorted them from England to the cemeteries where their loved ones lay. They also tended the graves of some of those whose relations couldn't travel and sent home pressed flowers, photographs, etc.

Ada continued with War Graves visitation until 1923, by which time most of the cemeteries had been taken over by the Imperial War Graves Commission (now the Commonwealth War Graves Commission), and furnished with the standard white headstones. She then returned to the Island and apart from short holidays in Jersey and England, never left it again. She worked as a private nurse/companion and married Walter James Bourgaize in 1928.

The couple ran Torteval Stores and during the occupation years of World War II (1940-45) put themselves in great danger by hiding British Commandos from Operation Ambassador in their loft. Ada and Walter had no children, but were happily married for over 50 years. Walter died in January 1983 and Ada just six months later aged 88.

Ada tending the grave of Private George Bougourd. The grave was one of those lost when the ground was fought over again. Private Bougourd RGLI is now commemorated on the Cambrai Memorial at Louverval.

Ada (right) and colleagues at Point du Jour Military Cemetery near Arras.

King George V (right) and General Haig, the British Commander in Chief, (left) inspecting an Honour Guard of the RGLI in 1917.

Acknowlegements

This publication offers only a snapshot of Guernsey and the Great War.

Guernsey Museums and Galleries is grateful for information supplied by: Liz Walton and The Channel Islands Great War Study Group. This group welcomes contributions and can be contacted through www.greatwarci.net.

Major Edwin Parks whose book 'Diex Aix: God Help Us-The Guernseymen who marched away 1914-1918' has detailed information on the RGLI in action.

The Guernsey Military History Company, a re-enactment group which aims to keep the spirit of the RGLI alive.

Text: David Mosley

Edited by: Lynne Ashton

Additional information:
Matt Harvey and Dr. Jason Monaghan

Images: Courtesy of the Imperial War Museum (IWM), Guernsey Museums & Galleries (GMAG/GMS), and Liz Walton

Additional drawings: Ann Segers

Design and Artwork: Bob Waite

Supported by:
The Rothschild Group in Guernsey

 ROTHSCHILD

 CULTURE AND LEISURE
A STATES OF GUERNSEY GOVERNMENT DEPA